THE GREAT BOOK A
LIONS

FOR KIDS

To Dudas,

May all your dreams come true.

The great Book about Lions ©2019
Text and illustrations by G. Guarita and Qwerty Books.
All rights reserved.
ISBN: 9781797563718

QWERTY BOOKS

A WORD FROM THE AUTHOR

From lions to lizards, from dolphins to dinosaurs, from space to how things work, all that and everything in between, fascinated me growing up.

In different ways, I was blessed with the priceless fortune of growing up in houses full of amazing books. I spent my childhood breathing stories in endless pages with amazing pictures, having fun learning wonderful and incomparable lessons that I have carried with me throughout my live and passed on to my children and students.

Because I love to teach what I learn, I wrote The Great Book About Lions, so you can learn, feel and have fun the same way that I learned, felt and had fun growing up surrounded by fascinating books.

So buckle up! It's time to discover The Great Book About Lions for Kids.

G. Guarita

Welcome to the amazing world of lions, beautiful and majestic creatures that conquered mankind's imagination since the dawn of times. Lions are powerful animals and expert hunters, but also loving and caring parents, and excellent team players.

In this book you will learn all about what makes lions such remarkable and legendary animals: you will learn about their size, weight, and strength; about their hunting abilities and habits; about their habitat, different species and extinct family members; and many more interesting facts, in this **Great Book About Lions**.

For all of their roaring, growling, and ferociousness, lions are family animals and truly social in their own communities. They usually live in groups of 15 or more animals, called prides. They also spend much of their time resting, sometimes staying inactive for up to 20 hours a day...

Prides can be as small as three or as big as 40 animals. As a tight family, lions hunt, raise cubs, and defend their territory together.

African lion prides consist of up to three males, around a dozen females, and their young. There are prides that have as many as 40 members, though.

LIONS & LIONS

In prides the females do most of the hunting and cub rearing. Usually all the lionesses in the pride are related: mothers, daughters, grandmothers, and sisters. Many of the females in the pride give birth at about the same time, and a cub may even nurse from other females as well as its mother.

Lionesses in a pride are usually related to each other, and tend to stay with the pride in which they are born. Males, on the other hand, wander off to create their own pride when they are old enough.

DID YOU KNOW?

The Lion is the only member of the big cat family that lives and hunts in groups, called prides.

Once, lions roared across most of Africa and parts of Asia and Europe. Nowadays lions mostly live in East and Southern Africa, inhabiting the open grasslands and savannahs where they share their habitat with the great herds of zebras and wildebeests, gazelles and oryx.

Lions are rarely found in dense forests, preferring grassy plains or open woodlands, with bushes and scattered Acacia trees serving as shade.

Present lion population distribution

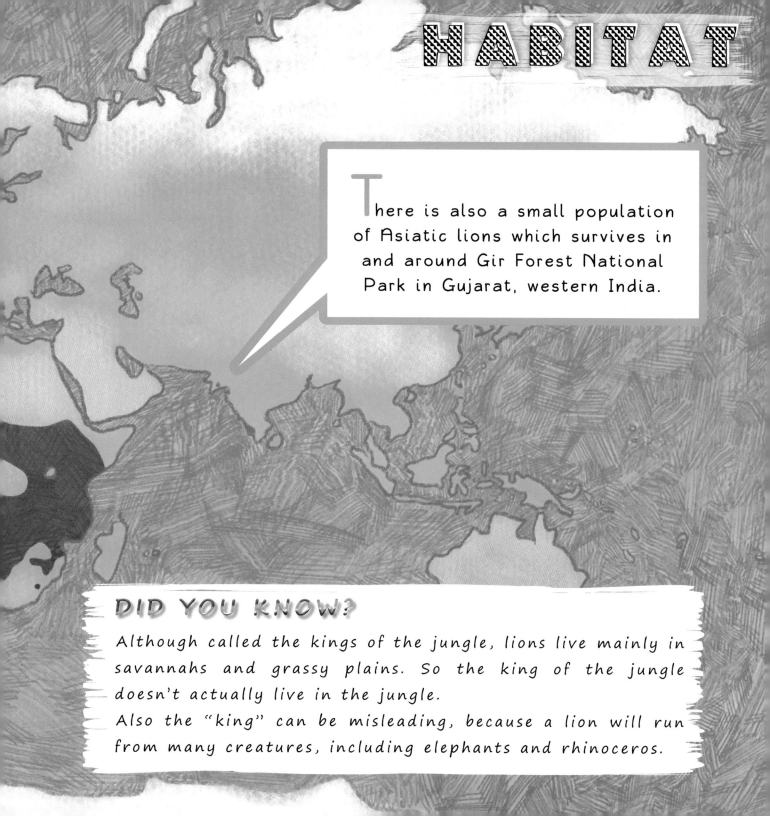

There is also a small population of Asiatic lions which survives in and around Gir Forest National Park in Gujarat, western India.

DID YOU KNOW?

Although called the kings of the jungle, lions live mainly in savannahs and grassy plains. So the king of the jungle doesn't actually live in the jungle.

Also the "king" can be misleading, because a lion will run from many creatures, including elephants and rhinoceros.

Lionesses give birth to a litter of one to 4 cubs, in a secure den, usually away from the pride.

A lioness nurses her still wet newborn babies, a few hours old.

The little babies are born blind, with dark spots on their bodies, and close to defenseless. But the cubs grow fast, on the second day they start crawling, and their eyes start to open within a week.

Newborn lion cub, just 4 days old.

Less than a month from being born, the lion cubs can now walk, and with six to eight weeks of age they are integrated with the pride.

A nursing female with sucking cubs.

A tight family.

Often pride lionesses have their babies at the same time, and cubs can even suckle from any of the nursing females.

MOMMIES AND CUBS

A patient lioness with three cubs.

The young lions soon begin to immerse themselves in the pride's life, playing among themselves, and with the adults. Often male adult lions patiently let the cubs play with their tail and mane.

Male lions reach adulthood at about 3 years, and are often forced to leave the pride and become nomads.

Lionesses usually remain with their birth pride, but they can also be forced to leave, when a pride becomes too large.

Lions are big and strong animals, and capable of running very fast, even if only in short bursts. So they usually prefer to slowly stalk their preys, getting as close as possible before starting the attack.

They usually hunt as a group, with lionesses (the female lions) doing most of the work. Males are typically solo hunters who prefer to ambush their prey.

Lions usually attempt to catch their prey with a fast rush and a final leap to the target.

These great hunters are usually more diurnal than other big cats, but also adapt to being active at night and at twilight.

Hunting is paramount in a lion's life, and training starts at an early age. For this young cub, even a raven is a perfect target to get some more practice.

Cape Buffalo

Onyx

Zebra

Lioness

Warthog

Wildebeest

Giraffe

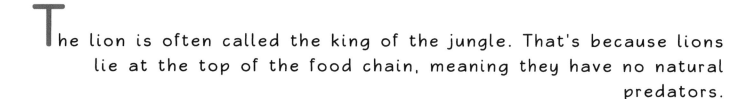

The lion is often called the king of the jungle. That's because lions lie at the top of the food chain, meaning they have no natural predators.

Lions are talented and skilled hunters, preying mainly on medium size mammals like wildebeest, zebra, buffalo, oryx and giraffe. They also prey on warthog, depending on their availability.

Lions usually avoid bigger animals like adult elephants, rhinoceroses and hippopotamus, as well as very small prey.

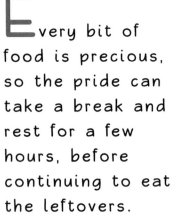

A meal is always a family event. The pride eats together, and everyone eat their fill, including old and injured lions.

Every bit of food is precious, so the pride can take a break and rest for a few hours, before continuing to eat the leftovers.

An adult male lion needs about 15 pounds (7 kg) of meat per day, but can eat as much as 66 pounds (30 kg) of food at a time. The amount needed for a female lion is about 11 pounds (5 kg) per day.

Did you know ?

A hyper-carnivore is an animal which has a diet that is more than 70% meat. Some examples of hyper-carnivores are crocodiles, eagles, dolphins, snakes, spiders, and of course, lions.

One of the most widely recognized animals, the lion belongs to the Felidae family, like tigers, jaguars, leopards and even our house cats.

THE LION'S BODY

The lion ('Panthera leo') possesses a deep chest, muscular frame, round ears and rounded head, and a little tuft of hair at the end of his tail.

Male lions can grow to 10 feet (3 meters) long, with their tales reaching up to 3 foot (1 meter). In terms of weight, they can reach 550 pounds (250 kilograms). Female lions are slightly smaller, at 9 feet (2.7 meters) in length and 395 pounds (180 kilograms) in weight.

Lions are extremely powerful, and use their muscles to deliver heavy blows that can break a zebra's back. While the average life for lions is 13 years, one lion in West Germany lived for 29 years!

2 meters

1 meter

0

0   1 meter   2 meters

(scale in meters, excluding the tail)

Lions have magnificent teeth which have evolved to kill (and eat!) their prey. The canine teeth of the mighty lion are cleverly spaced to fit perfectly between prey's vertebrae. Meanwhile, their back teeth act like a pair of scissors and this allows them to cut their meat is smaller chunks while eating.

The tail serves a key purpose for these big cats: it helps them to stay balanced while jumping or running at high speeds, and is also used as a signal during group hunts. Small lion cubs also look for the tassel of their mum's tail to know where to go.

Thanks to the delicate pads on their paws, lions can be very very silent when moving around. This allows them to get really close to their prey, quietly and without being detected.

Lions claws retract into the paw when they aren't needed and this keeps them sharp until they are needed. This also prevents them from hurting each other. This is important because a lion's claw can grow to one and a half inches, or 38mm!

Lions have a fantastic sense of smell; they can smell nearby prey while also guessing how new the smell is to the area. They also use scent deposits to mark their territory. When another predator spots a lion's kill, only the bravest will attempt to steal it because they can smell the lion's mark.

A male African lion sniffing at the ground

A young lion swivels its ears, enabling him to hear distant sounds, and pinpoint their origins.

Their hearing is above average compared to others in the animal kingdom and this is aided by their ability to swivel both ears. Not only can they hear distant sounds, they can pinpoint the location of the sound too!

Their eyesight is where they really excel and it's actually FIVE TIMES stronger than our own eyesight. With larger eyes than many similar-sized animals, their pupils are round and this makes them a visual animal. Although they can't move their eyes (they have to move their whole head), their eyes work brilliantly in low light and this is why they are such efficient night hunters!

Did You Know?

As many nocturnal animals, lions' eyes glow in the dark because of a layer called the **tapetum lucidum**, a reflective surface behind their retinas. It increases their sensitivity to light, helping them to see better in low light.

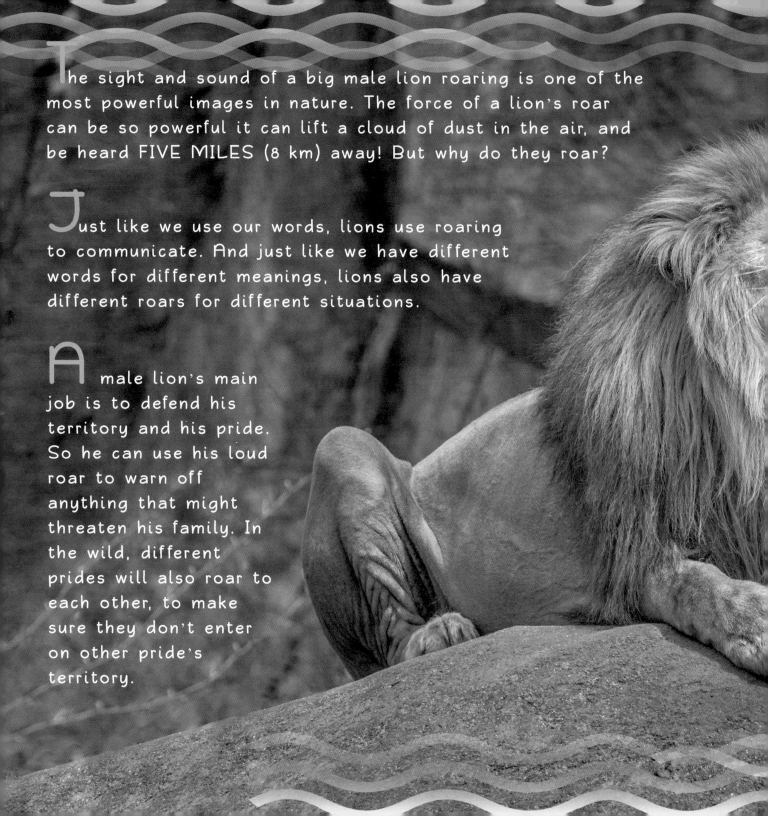

The sight and sound of a big male lion roaring is one of the most powerful images in nature. The force of a lion's roar can be so powerful it can lift a cloud of dust in the air, and be heard FIVE MILES (8 km) away! But why do they roar?

Just like we use our words, lions use roaring to communicate. And just like we have different words for different meanings, lions also have different roars for different situations.

A male lion's main job is to defend his territory and his pride. So he can use his loud roar to warn off anything that might threaten his family. In the wild, different prides will also roar to each other, to make sure they don't enter on other pride's territory.

THE LION'S ROAR

Lions also use roars to communicate with another lions. And each lion makes a slightly different sound, or oof, which helps them recognize one another.

Lionesses use a very gentle roar when calling for their cubs, and even the big males use a softer roar when playing with their young.

Did You Know?

The term "big cat" is typically used to refer to any of the five members of the genus Panthera, namely tiger, lion, jaguar, leopard, and snow leopard. Except for snow leopards, these cats are the only ones who are able to roar.

It is thought that the main purpose of the mane is to protect the lion's neck and throat in fights.

From all the lion's physical traits, the mane is probably the most distinctive. A male lion in his prime, with a grand and bushy mane, rarely fails to impress.

THE LION'S MANE

A lion's mane is typically brownish and tinged with yellow, rust and black hairs. It starts growing when lions are about a year old, and tends to grow bigger and darker with age. Mane hair is firm and wiry, like stiff horsehair.

Lion cubs are born without mane

The extent of the mane varies from lion to lion, with some having no mane at all, while others have a luxurious mane that runs onto the body, along the abdomen, and even onto the fronts of the back legs.

Young male African lions, just starting to grow their manes.

Research shows that its color and size are influenced by factors such as temperature. Some lions from the Serengeti and North Africa have a nearly black mane, while Asiatic lions usually have sparser manes or can even be maneless.

Adult Asiatic lions usually have a sparser mane than their African cousins

Lions are cats, members of the feline (Felidae) family, which includes among others the cheetah, puma, jaguar, leopard, lynx, tiger, and the domestic cat.

DOMESTIC CAT

IBERIAN LYNX

SNOW LEOPARD

CHEETAH

The lion's closest relatives are the other species of the genus Panthera; the tiger, the snow leopard, the jaguar, and the leopard.

JAGUAR

TIGER

LEOPARD

BARBARY LION
(Algeria, 1893)

Lions evolved about one million years ago in Africa, and from there they diversified into a number of subspecies, such as the Barbary lion of North Africa, the Cave lion of Europe, the American lion of North and Central America, and the Asiatic lion of the Middle East and India.

CAVE LIONS
(Reconstruction)

AMERICAN LION
(Reconstruction)

Since then, several subspecies have become extinct, like the American and Cave lions, and possibly the Barbary lion. In the present days lions numbers have dwindled to a few tens of thousands, and those outside national parks are rapidly losing their habitat to agriculture.

While traditionally twelve recent subspecies of lion were recognized, recently this classification was revised by the IUCN, to include only two subspecies.

Panthera leo leo - includes the Asiatic, West African and Central African lion populations.

THE LION'S FAMILY

Panthera leo melanochaita - includes the East and Southern African lion populations.

DID YOU KNOW?

IUCN stands for International Union for Conservation of Nature. It is the global authority on the status of the natural world and the measures needed to safeguard it.

The mysterious white lion varies from blond to near white. These lions are not albinos. Instead, their white color is the result of a rare color mutation.

Regarded as divine by local populations, this color variant shows up only once in a while, especially in the Timbavati region of South Africa.

Unlike true albino animals (like the white tiger), white lions' coloration doesn't seem to be a disadvantage to their survival. Several white lions have been reintroduced into their natural habitat and have been hunting and breeding successfully for a significant amount of time.

how cute am I?

White lions range from near white to blond, like these lionesses.

THE WHITE LION

Did you know?

The coat color of a lion is not determined so much by the color of the hair, but by the ratio of light-colored hairs to dark-colored hairs.

Lions are seen as strong but noble creatures, often called "the king of the jungle". They have been a popular symbol of royalty and greatness, as well as a symbol of bravery.

The earliest known cave paintings of lions were found in the Chauvet Cave and in Lascaux in France, dating more than 30,000 years ago.

In ancient Mesopotamia, lions were a symbol of force and were kept and bred by Assyrian kings. The Babylonian goddess Ishtar was represented driving a chariot drawn by seven lions.

In ancient Egypt, the lion was a symbol of power and kingship. Sekhmet, depicted as a lioness, was the goddess of love and the patron and protector of the people, the king, and the land.

The Chinese Imperial guardian lions, or Shishi, are traditional stone ornaments. A pair of lions statues are thought to protect homes from harmful spirits. Their use is spread to most parts of Asia.

Lions also feature in ancient Greek mythology, like in the myth of the Nemean lion, believed to be a supernatural lion that occupied the sacred town of Nemea.

Cave art paintings in the Chauvet Cave, France

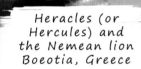

Heracles (or Hercules) and the Nemean lion Boeotia, Greece

Statue of Sekhmet from the temple of Mut

Lion from the Ishtar Gate, originally built in Babylon, Iraq (now shown in Berlin's Pergamon Museum)

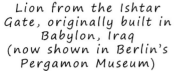

Stone Chinese guardian lion at Mount Emei, China

The lion has been an icon used by humanity for thousands of years, but nowadays, its story is not so cheerful.

The latest IUCN studies estimate 23,000-39,000 lions are living in the wild. It may seem like a lot, but their numbers are rapidly decreasing, by almost half every 20 years. The species is now listed as Vulnerable on the IUCN

Humans continue to expand their farmland, and this not only reduces lions' hunting territory, but also leads to clashes between the cats and the locals. Many times ending up in the death of the lion by the farmer, who is trying to protect his livestock. Poaching also posts a big threat to the majestic cats.

CONSERVATION

Lions are top predators, and play a crucial role in keeping a healthy balance in nature. Lions usually take down the weakest of the herd. This keeps the herd population resilient and healthy.

Lions also help to keep the equilibrium of numbers among other animals, especially herbivores like buffalo, zebra and wildebeest, which in turn influences the condition of grasslands and forests.

By protecting a lion's landscape, we're helping the whole area to thrive, which doesn't just benefit wildlife but the people who rely on local natural resources too.

Did you know ?

Simba is the Swahili word for lion. But it also means "king", "strong", and "aggressive". The perfect word to describe a lion.

Photo Credits

Front Page – Peter Fischer/Pixabay
From The Author – Ian Lindsay/Pixabay
Index – Christine Sponchia/Pixabay
Hunting – Tambako The Jaguar/Flickr; Damien Ramos/Flickr; Demetrius John Kessy/Flickr
A Lion's Meal – Charles J. Sharp/Wikimedia; Vecteezy.Com; Katja/Pixabay; Zgmorris13/Pixabay; Kirsi Kataniemi/Pixabay
A Lion's Meal (2nd Page) – Justin Hall/Pixabay; Marcel Langthim/Pixabay; Guldem Ustun/Flickr
Lions & Lions – Les Bohlen/Pixabay; Sue Brady/Pixabay; Stoiber Christian/Pixabay; Gwen/Pixabay; Ranit Kumar Dholey/Wikimedia
Lion's Body - Rabe/Pixabay
Lion's Body (2nd Page) – Gerhild Klinkow/Pixabay; Frans Van Heerden/Pexels; Cookie Overbeek/Pixabay; Eric Kilby/Flickr
The Lion's Roar – Fred Faulkner/Flickr; Margo Tanenbaum/Pixabay
Senses – David Clode/Unsplash; Bernard Dupont/Flickr; Silvia/Pixabay
Lion's Mane - Alexandra/Pixabay; Vanisri874/Wikipedia; Ian Lindsay/Pixabay; Miroslav Duchacek/Wikipedia; Pxhere
White Lion - Kristie/Pixabay; Gerald Friedrich/Pixabay
Mommies And Cubs – Angie Gottling/Pixabay; Tambako The Jaguar/Flickr; Irina Anastasiv/Pexels; Sharon Sipple/Flickr; Fernando Prado/Pixabay; Karen Alchin/Pexels
The Lion's Family – Brian Gratwicke/Flickr; Kandukuru Nagarjun/Flickr; Ashley Coates/Flickr; Vickey Chauhan/Wikimedia; Pexels/Pixabay; Gregory Slobirdr Smith/Flickr; Michael Siebert/Pixabay
Evolution – Gerhard Bogner/Pixabay; Programa Ex-Situ Conservação Do Lince Ibérico; Marcel Langthim/Pixabay; DrZoltan/Pixabay; Fxxu/Pixabay; Michael Siebert/Pixabay; Alfred Edward Pease/Wikimedia; Mauricio Antón/Wikimedia; NPS Photo
Lions And Us – Tim Tentcher/Pixabay; Bibi Saint-Pol/Wikimedia; McLeod/Wikimedia; Miguel Hermoso Cuesta/Wikimedia; HTO/Wikimedia
Conservation - Eliza/Pixabay; Carch/Pixabay; Jensfriislund/Pixabay; Roman Boed/Flickr; lifeforstock/Freepik

Printed in Great Britain
by Amazon